# An Adult Fairy Tale

## Harold Forward

Forward Children's Book—Waco, TX
ISBN: 978-0-578-78231-7
Library of Congress Control Number: 2020920676
Title: An Adult Fairy Tale
Author: Harold Forward
Digital distribution | 2020
Paperback | 2020

This is a work of fiction. The characters, names, incidents, places, and dialogue are products of the author's imagination, and are not to be construed as real.

# Dedication

To help you look behind the mask...

There was a wealthy young lady.

She was bored with life, so she decided to travel the world.

The lady bought a yacht, learned everything about the sea, and decided to sail.

She had been on the calm sea for about a month.

Then this day, all of a sudden, dark clouds rose from the horizon.

Those clouds turned into a storm, the winds roared, and the rain fell hard. The boat tossed back-and-forth vigorously.

She then decided to pray.
   She said, "Lord if you let me make it out of this
storm, I'll be grateful."

The storm got worse. The wind broke the boat apart, and it started to sink.

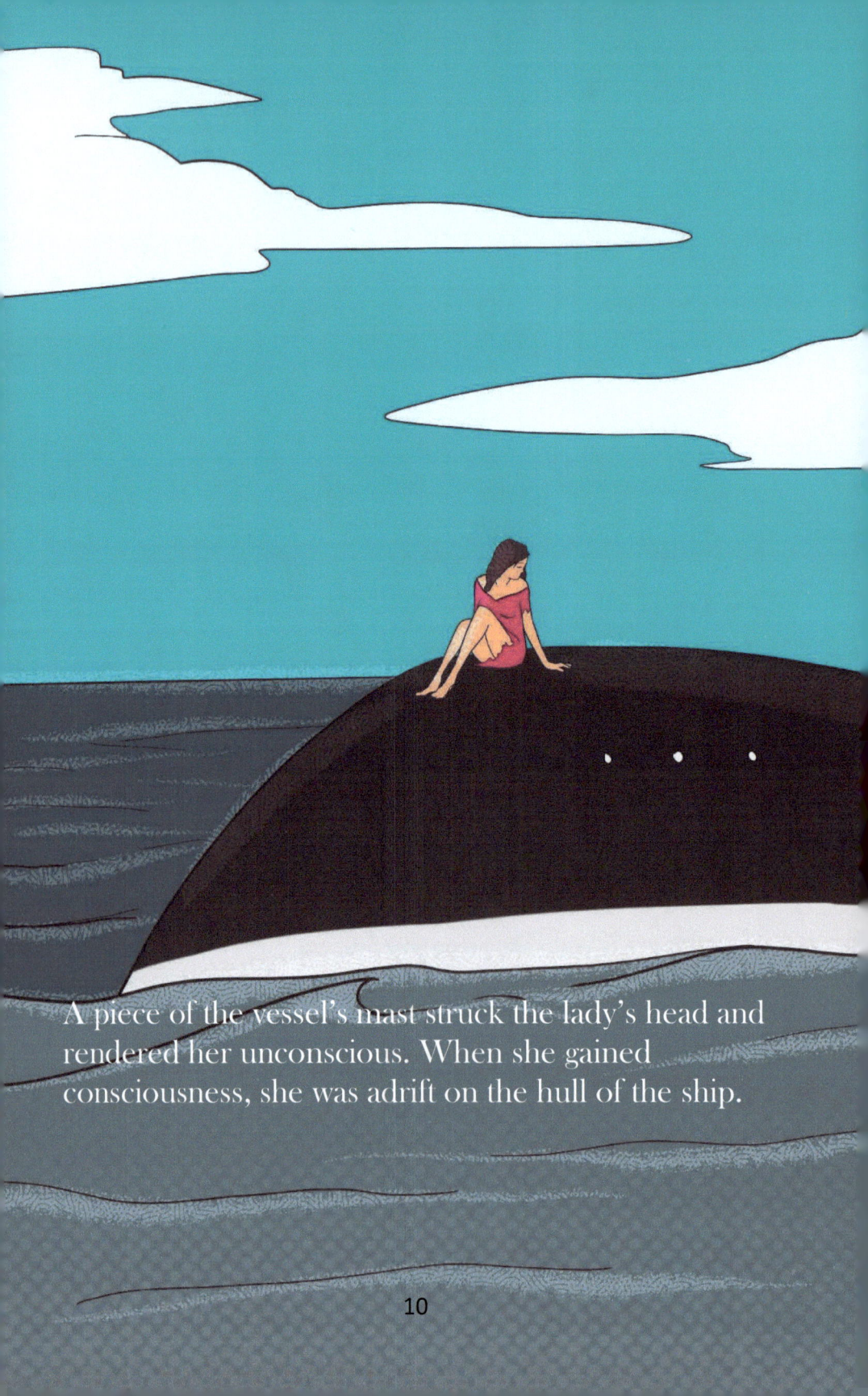

A piece of the vessel's mast struck the lady's head and rendered her unconscious. When she gained consciousness, she was adrift on the hull of the ship.

She said humbly, "Father, I'm thankful for my life, but, if only I had dry land beneath my feet."

As soon as she stopped praying, a small island appeared on the horizon.

She paddled on her back to the island.
She decided to make the best
of this and called it home.

One year, two years, then several years passed. She looked upon God once again.

"Lord, if only I had someone I could talk to, I'm so lonely."

And yet soon as the words came out of her mouth, a little small cute monkey was in the top of a palm tree, grunting and squeaking.

She was happy and tried to become friends with the monkey. She begged him to come down, she decided to give him food, but the monkey kept its distance.

She thought, "Maybe in time it'll get better."

She attempted for months to get closer to this monkey, but it would throw coconuts at her. Some coconuts would hurt her! So, she decided to be grateful for his friendship.

She thought, "*I love him for who he is and keep my distance.*"

More time had passed.

She was walking the beach one day and saw a ship on the horizon.

She quickly made a distress fire. Hoping they would see and save her.

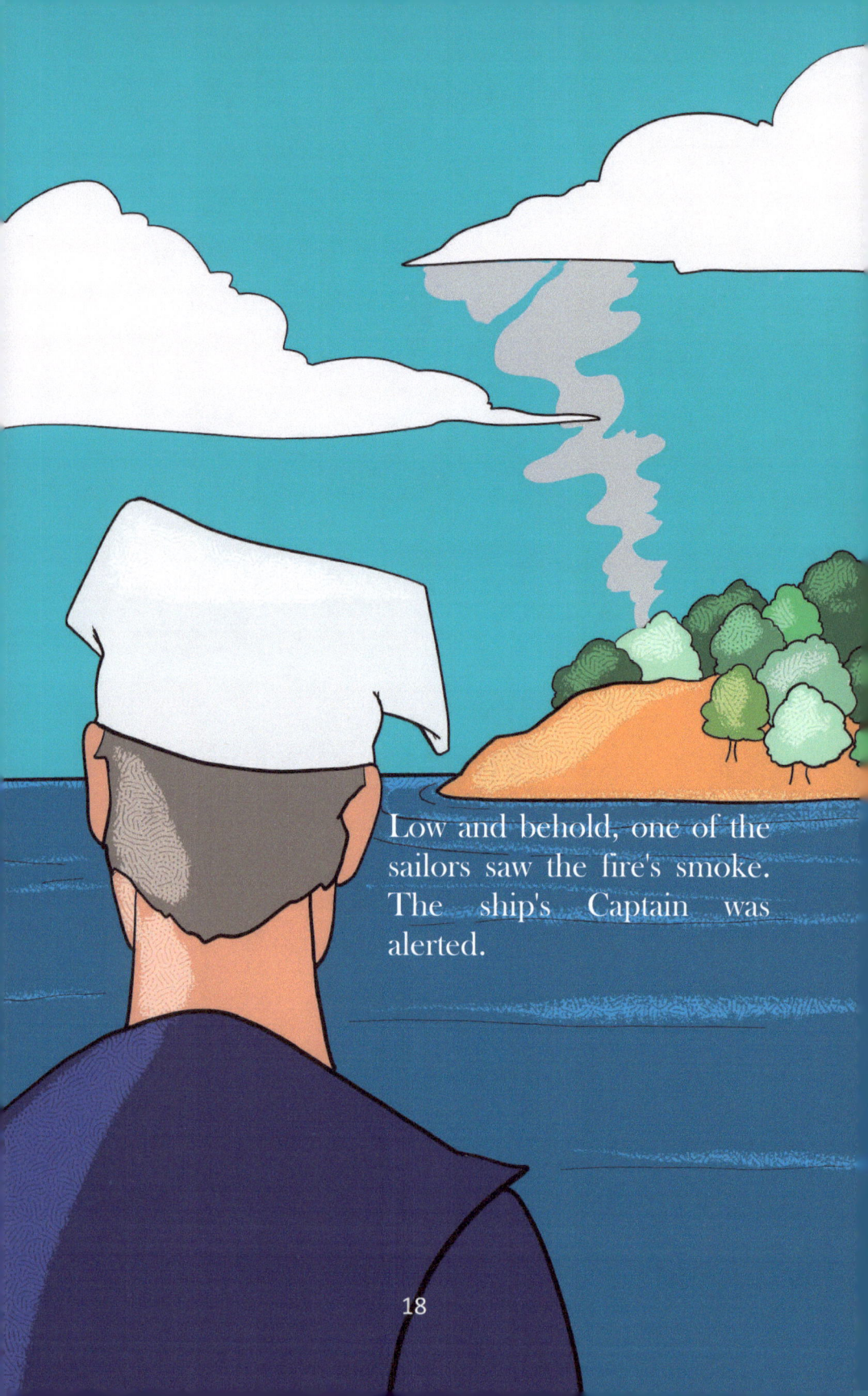

Low and behold, one of the sailors saw the fire's smoke. The ship's Captain was alerted.

With a small crew, the Captain rowed to the island. By following the smoke, they discovered her and asked her name.

He told her that everyone thought she had died. Her business fortune had doubled. He offered her the best accommodations on his ship. The Captain wanted to reunite her with her family and home; she was happy.

She hurriedly gathered her things. As she stepped into the dinghy, she told the Captain, "I got a friend here. Can he come with us too?"

The Captain said, "Sure!"

She pointed up in the palm tree.

The Captain said, "I don't see anyone. I only see a monkey."

She answered, "That's him!"

The Captain replied, "That isn't a person!"

She pleaded with the Captain.

21

The lady became upset and said, "I can't leave him; he was the only friend I had for several years. I'm accustomed to him and genuinely love him. We shouldn't just leave him!"

He then sent his crew to get the monkey down from the palm tree. The monkey threw coconuts at the sailors and injured them.

The Captain told the lady, "I am sorry, but he won't come."

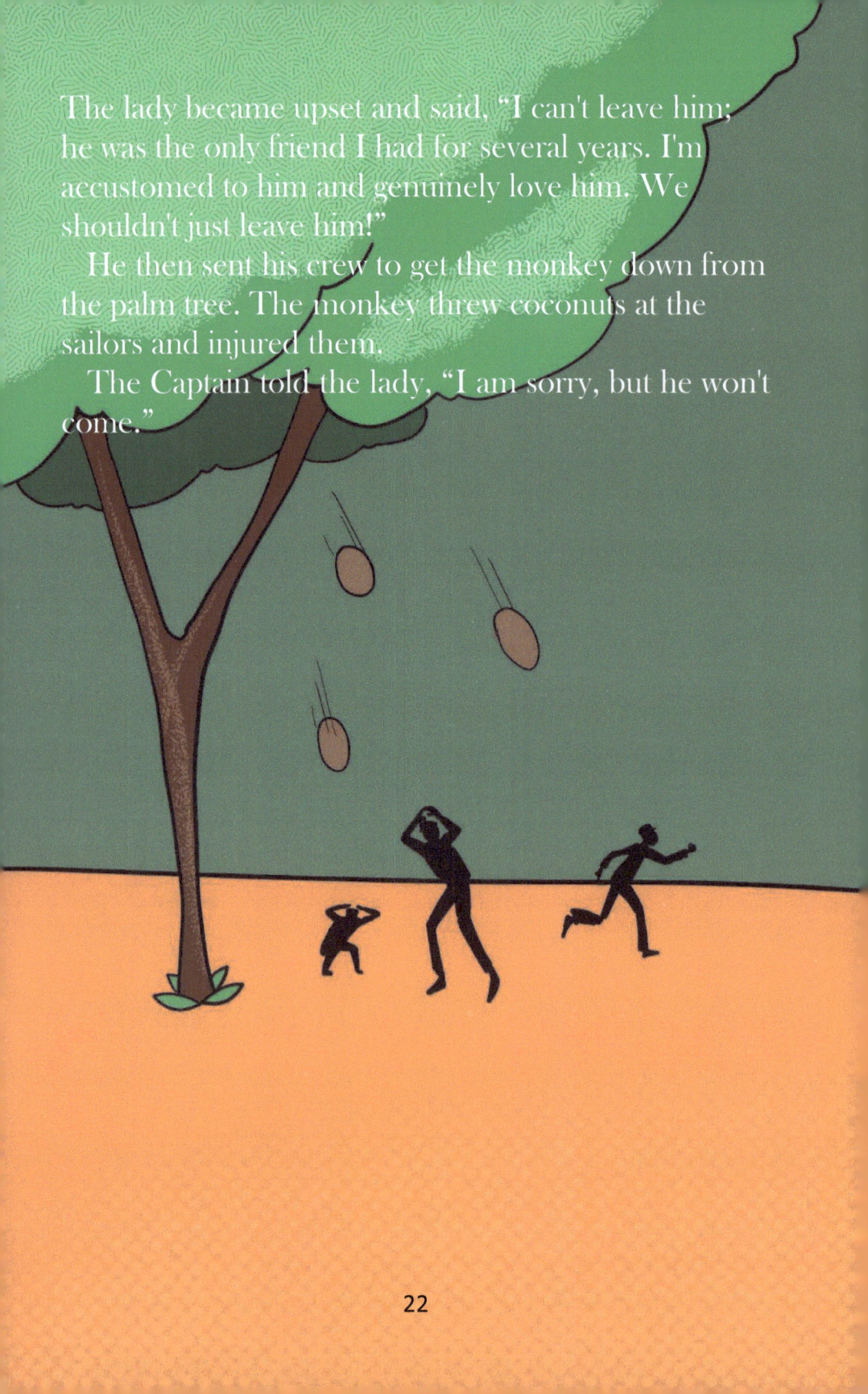

The Captain told her, "You got to understand! He's an animal! It's just his nature to be difficult. You and he are so different! If you can't tame him, we can't either. So, come and leave this monkey on this island."

She told the Captain, "I guess I will stay."

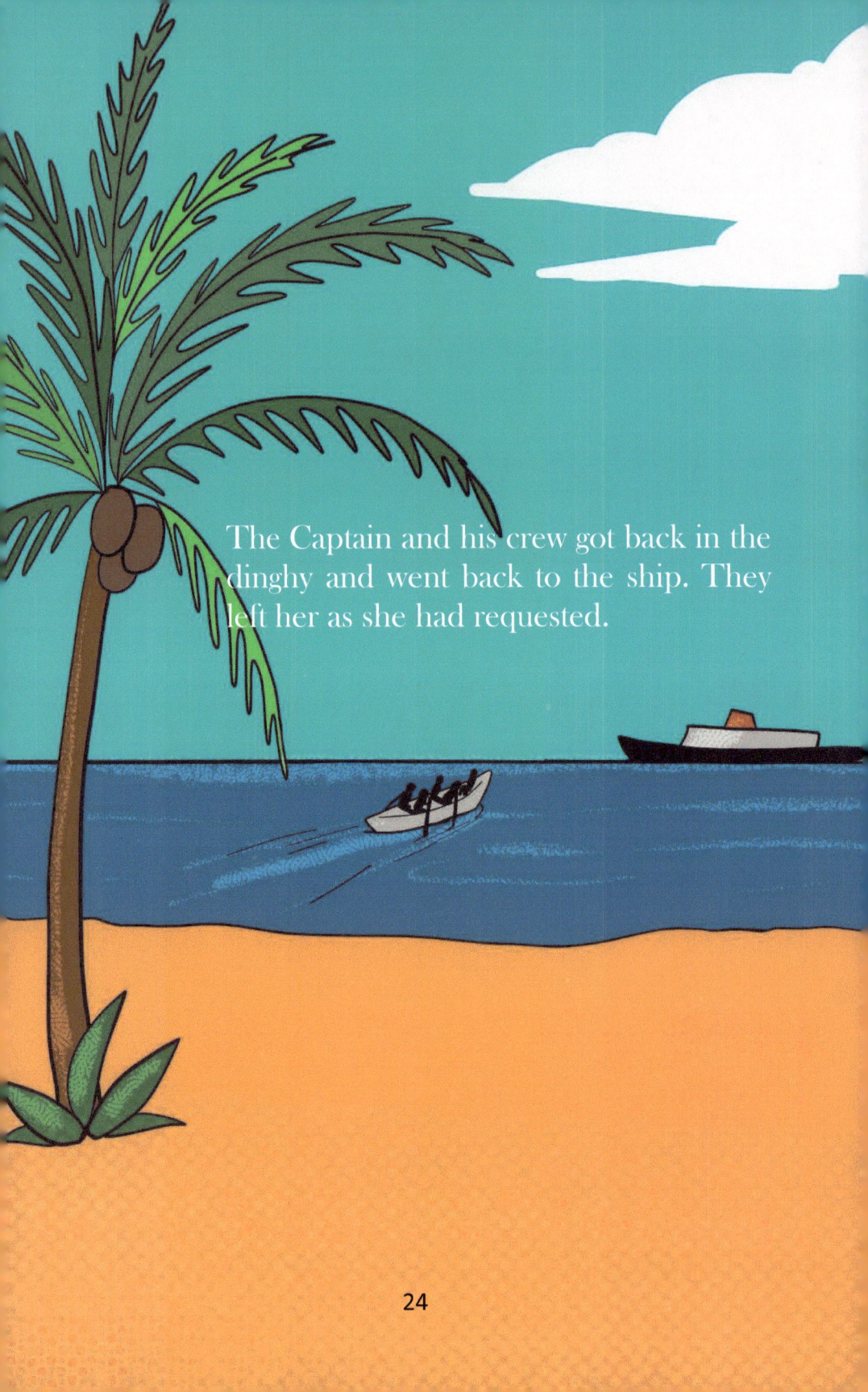

The Captain and his crew got back in the dinghy and went back to the ship. They left her as she had requested.

The moral of the story is that I'M THE CAPTAIN and domestic violence isn't a fairy tale! I'm trying to help you to leave this place and leave your monkey.

No matter what you feel, no matter what you have been through, he will always keep you at a distance. You can't tame or change him.

He will have you isolated here from family, friends, and a better life. You will be staying with someone you don't understand and doesn't understand you.

You call me because he oppresses you! He will not be obsessed, possessed, or controlled by anyone! You just need to leave.

Tomorrow, his face will show remorse and hurt, but he's an animal on the inside. You need to see a monkey's face whenever you look into his eyes. So leave him here, and let me show you what you are missing!

# About the Author

Harold H. Forward is an aspring writer, amateur photographer, and entrepreneur. He retired with 40 years of combined experience as a law-enforcement officer for the military and a metropolitan city. His children's books are born out of the love for emotional growth and support. He's also the author of the beautiful children's book, My Star. Forward's hometown is Waco, Texas and he is currently living in Dallas.